Specifiers' Handbooks for Inclusive Design

Automatic Door Systems

This guide has been produced by the Centre for Accessible Environments
in conjunction with RIBA Enterprises.

Text and drawings by Alison Grant MA Arch RIBA NRAC Consultant
Case studies researched and compiled by Paul Highman

Published: January 2005

© Centre for Accessible Environments and RIBA Enterprises, 2005

ISBN 1 85946 171 9
Stock Code 37725

Centre for Accessible Environments
70 South Lambeth Road
London SW8 1RL

Tel/textphone: +44 (0)20 7840 0125
Fax: +44 (0)20 7840 5811
Email: info@cae.org.uk
Website: www.cae.org.uk

The Centre for Accessible Environments is a Company Limited by Guarantee
registered in England and Wales No 3112684, Registered Charity No 1050820.

RIBA Enterprises
15 Bonhill Street
London EC2P 2EA

Tel: +44 (0)20 7496 8300
Fax: +44 (0)20 7374 8200
Email: sales@ribabooks.com
Website: www.ribabookshops.com

RIBA Enterprises is a Company Limited by Guarantee registered in England and Wales No 978271.

Designed by Steve Paveley Design
Typeset by Academic + Technical Typesetting, Bristol
Printed and bound by Latimer Trend, Plymouth

Foreword

One of the key elements in meeting the various forms of building legislation and standards in force today, including the stringent requirements of the Disability Discrimination Act, is the provision of safe and effective access to buildings. Having said that, it should be remembered that creating an accessible entrance from the street is only the beginning of the task. Disabled people should be able to move freely and conveniently throughout the entire building. This requires that doorways between rooms, those leading to corridors and into toilets and lift areas can be negotiated with ease, and central to providing such freedom of movement is the provision of correctly identified door types and access controls.

As one of the world's leading suppliers of door technology systems and allied products operating internationally in 44 countries, the company for which I work, DORMA, can help in all these situations and would seem a natural candidate to sponsor this guide. Undoubtedly, in terms of technical ability this is certainly true, but DORMA's approach goes way beyond just the provision of technically advanced products. We would lay a stronger claim. Technical ability alone does not make a company professional,

it simply makes it competent. Professionalism means offering practical, often impartial advice on the different types of automatic door system available and the factors affecting design and specification – plus the assurance that our knowledge of the latest issues affecting legislation, building regulations and standards is totally current. We even practise what we preach. Our new bespoke UK headquarters, at Hitchin in Hertfordshire, has provided DORMA with the perfect opportunity to integrate a host of its own products, including ironmongery for manual doors, into a 'showcase' working environment. Early in the planning stage we undertook a full access audit and developed a strategy to meet the various potential challenges to best practice presented by the new 7,500m^2 three-storey building and adjoining warehouse.

DORMA is delighted to be associated with this excellent CAE/RIBA Enterprises publication, which should prove invaluable to a very wide audience.

Simon Chapman
DDA Product Specialist
DORMA UK Ltd

Acknowledgements

We are grateful to DORMA UK Limited for sponsorship of this guide and for providing photographs and text for the case studies.

Contents

Introduction

Specifiers' Handbooks series

The *Specifiers' Handbooks for Inclusive Design* series comprises a set of design guides which look in detail at the technical aspects of key building elements. The series expands on guidance in *Designing for Accessibility*, a leading CAE/RIBA Enterprises publication covering inclusive design in a range of public buildings.

The *Specifiers' Handbooks for Inclusive Design* series has been prepared to assist designers, specifiers, building owners and occupiers, building managers and facilities managers to understand key design aspects and characteristics of specific architectural elements. The series combines technical guidance with informative case studies, designed to facilitate a practical understanding of the element in focus. The first three handbooks in the series cover:

- Platform lifts
- Architectural ironmongery
- Automatic door systems

The information in the handbooks should assist people responsible for the selection and specification of each architectural element to make decisions which will lead to the procurement of the most suitable product.

The information will also assist people who are responsible for ongoing maintenance to understand the importance of regular checks and the implications for disabled and other people if equipment is taken out of action for any reason.

About this handbook

Automatic Door Systems covers detailed aspects of automatic door systems, including automatic sliding, folding, swing and balanced doors and low-energy swing doors, for use in non-domestic buildings.

The handbook offers practical guidance to help specifiers understand the different types of automatic door system available, the factors contributing to their design and specification, and related legislation, building regulations and standards. The design guidance is supported by case study examples which illustrate different types of system in a range of situations.

Doors fitted with automatic systems may also require conventional door ironmongery, such as lever handles, pull handles, locks and latches. These items are covered in detail in another handbook in the series: *Architectural Ironmongery*.

The legislative framework

Building Regulations

Automatic door systems may be installed as an integral part of a new development and where improvements are being made to doors in existing buildings. All new developments will be subject to approval under the Building Regulations, in which case the provisions in the relevant Approved Document, Technical Standard or Technical Booklet will be applicable. Depending on the nature and extent of building improvements, approval under the Building Regulations may or may not be required.

England and Wales

Approved Document M 2004 Edition *Access to and use of buildings* (AD M) incorporates provisions relating to the installation of automatic door systems, referred to in Section 2 as 'powered entrance doors'. The objective of the provisions is to:

- provide an accessible entrance(s) to the building, whether a new or an existing building, and
- minimise the risks to people when entering a building

For an entrance to be deemed 'accessible', a number of provisions are established, including the following, in section 2.13a:

'Where required to be self-closing, a power operated door opening and closing system is used when through calculation and experience it appears that it will not be possible otherwise for a person to open the door using a force no greater that 20N at the leading edge.'

Powered entrance doors satisfy Requirements M1 and M2 by incorporating:

- automatic sensors to control door movement
- safety devices to ensure doors do not close on a person positioned in the doorway
- a fail-safe mechanism in the event of a power failure
- suitable controls positioned in an accessible location

All these aspects are discussed in detail in the *Practical Guidance* section.

Automatic door systems are also referred to in Section 3 of AD M as a design consideration in relation to internal doors, primarily as a means of overcoming the force required to open doors fitted with self-closing devices.

Scotland

Technical Standard S refers to the use of automatic controls for entrance and internal doors and the provision of an adjacent side-hinged or automatic door, where an entrance comprises a revolving door.

Northern Ireland

Technical Booklet R refers to the use of automatic controls for entrance and internal doors, and discourages the use of revolving doors except large revolving doors, which may be suitable in certain situations.

A more detailed discussion of the Building Regulations is included in the Appendices.

Disability Discrimination Act 1995

Internal and external doors and their associated ironmongery and control systems are considered to be a 'physical feature' under the Disability Discrimination Act 1995 (DDA).

- The installation of an automatic or powered door-opening device may be proposed to overcome an existing barrier to access, for example a heavy entrance door or doors along a corridor route. In this situation, the door control system will constitute a 'reasonable adjustment', designed to remove existing or potential barriers and promote equitable access.
- Conversely, the inappropriate use of an automatic door system, or the placement of controls in an inaccessible location, may itself create a physical barrier. In such situations, it may be appropriate for employers, service providers and providers of post-16 education to consider making adjustments to remove or alter the barrier in response to their duties under the Act.

The extent and nature of any adjustment will depend on the particular characteristics of the existing door or control system and on other factors such as practicality, the extent of disruption, the effectiveness of the adjustment and cost. The duty is to make **reasonable** adjustments, having taken into account all the relevant factors.

Duties under the DDA relate not only to the adjustment of physical features. They also relate to policies, practices and procedures, all of which could have a significant effect on the accessibility and usability of an existing automatic door system.

- For example, a service provider may have a policy which says that a powered door-opening mechanism should be switched off at a certain time each day in order to save energy. However, this could make access very difficult for a person visiting the building outside these specified hours. The service provider, in this scenario, is likely to be responding appropriately to duties under the DDA if they modify their policy to ensure that the powered door system is operational whenever the building is open to the public.

The DDA does not place duties on product designers and manufacturers in relation to the type of products, packaging or instructions they offer, on the basis that they do not involve the provision of a 'service' direct to the general public. Designers and manufacturers themselves have no duties under the Act to produce, for example, door control systems which are suitable for disabled customers. However, employers, service providers and providers of post-16 education who are responding to their duties to make reasonable adjustments will want to procure products and equipment that are designed to maximise accessibility and meet the needs of a broad range of customers. Manufacturers of products such as automatic door systems will clearly be designing products and controls suitable for disabled people, albeit on a market-led basis.

Further details on the Disability Discrimination Act 1995 are included in the Appendices.

Design and specification guidelines

British Standards

A number of British Standards are applicable to the design, installation and operation of automatic doors systems, the most relevant being:

BS 7036:1996 *Code of practice for safety at powered doors for pedestrian use*

    Part 1: General
    Part 2: Straight and curved sliding doors
            and prismatic and folding doors
    Part 3: Swing doors and balanced doors
    Part 4: Low-energy swing doors
    Part 5: Revolving doors

BS 7036 provides guidance to manufacturers, suppliers, installers, specifiers, occupiers and property owners on the provision, installation, safe operation and maintenance of automatic door systems, with particular reference to safety and avoiding risk of accident.

Another relevant British Standard is BS 8300:2001 *Design of buildings and their approaches to meet the needs of disabled people – Code of practice*. This document explains how the built environment can be designed to anticipate and overcome restrictions that prevent disabled people from making full use of premises and their surroundings.

Many of the design recommendations in BS 8300 are based for the first time on ergonomic research commissioned in 1997 and 2001 by the Department of the Environment, Transport and the Regions. BS 8300 includes commentary which provides a context and rationale for the design guidance. Management and maintenance issues are incorporated in recognition of the essential role these play in ensuring the accessibility of services and facilities to disabled people.

The recommendations in the standard apply to car parking provision, setting-down points and garaging, access routes to and around all buildings, and entrances to and interiors of new buildings. They inform the design guidance in AD M of the Building Regulations. They may also be used to assess the accessibility and usability of existing buildings and, where practicable, as a basis for their improvement.

Design issues

In many situations, automatic door systems will provide an ideal solution to the barriers otherwise presented by internal and external doors. Advances in technology and continuing innovation by manufacturers have led to the development of a wide range of systems to suit every possible scenario.

The selection and specification of automatic door systems is a specialist area owing to the complex technical characteristics and broad range of systems available. Anyone considering the procurement and installation of an automatic door system should seek specialist advice from the manufacturers. In many situations, the advice of the fire and building control authorities may also be relevant.

Selection of the most suitable type of automatic door system for a particular building will depend on the likely use and purpose of the door. Relevant user characteristics will include the volume and type of pedestrian traffic, environmental conditions such as wind exposure, whether use is continuous or intermittent, and whether the door is designated as an emergency exit route.

Some automatic door systems such as sliding, folding and balanced doors are installed as complete door systems. That is, the automatic system and controls are integral with the door leaves and framing. Such systems are available in a wide range of finishes including colour powder coating, stainless steel and aluminium. Alternatively, automatic door systems such as automatic swing doors and low-energy door operators can be retrofitted (or fitted as new) to solid timber door leaves or other existing doorsets.

Practical guidance

The following sections cover general design issues which are common to all types of automatic door system.

Planning

The size and configuration of any door fitted with an automatic door system should be considered alongside the space and arrangement of the surrounding features.

For example:

- Sufficient space should be provided on both sides of the door to accommodate the number of people expected to use the door.
- The doors should be located where they are clearly visible from the approach routes on both sides.
- Ramped floors to either side of an automatic door present a particular hazard and should be avoided.
- The plan layout of the doors and its surroundings should be designed to suit the expected level of pedestrian traffic.
- The approach routes to and from the door should be free of obstructions which could disrupt the flow of pedestrians. Obstructions might include permanent features such as rails, posts and benches as well as temporary items such as queuing rails and printed notices.
- Cross-flow of pedestrian routes near to the door should be avoided.
- If any doors are designed to be one-way, they should be clearly marked as such.

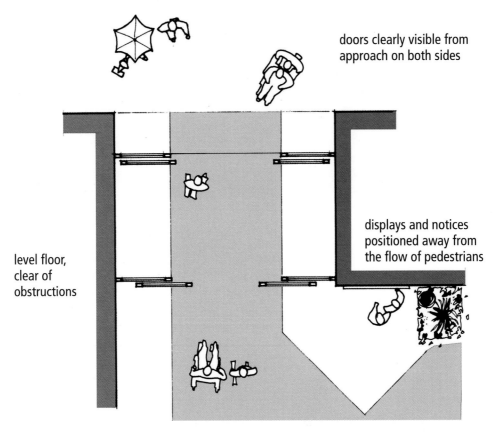

doors clearly visible from approach on both sides

displays and notices positioned away from the flow of pedestrians

level floor, clear of obstructions

ensure adequate space on both sides of door for expected number of people

*Figure 1 **Automatic door planning – design issues***

Door detail

Doors fitted with automatic door systems should either be fully glazed, or incorporate a vision panel which is sufficiently large to enable a person in both a seated and standing position to see and be seen from either side of the door. Large areas of glass can be confusing and present a hazard to many building users, particularly visually impaired people. Large glass panels in doors and screens should be clearly highlighted by the use of manifestation markings.

- Vision panels in solid doors should provide a minimum zone of visibility between 500mm and 1500mm above floor level. Where a horizontal mid-rail is required to the door leaf, the zone of visibility can be in two bands with minimum dimensions of 500–800mm and 1150–1500mm above floor level (see *Figure 2*).
- Manifestation markings should be provided to clearly highlight the presence of glass in doors and side screens. Markings should be provided at two heights (see *Figure 3*) and should contrast with the background surfaces when viewed through the door in both directions.
- To avoid the potential for hands and feet being trapped, the lower edge of any door fitted with an automatic door system should be installed with a minimal clearance from

the floor surface. The floor should also be even and level.

- To reduce the risk of tripping, any floor-mounted items, such as threshold plates, should be installed flush with the adjacent floor surface, or incorporate a shallow ramped edge.

Activation devices

Automatic door systems can be activated in a number of different ways.

Motion sensor – These comprise either radar or passive infrared sensors which are installed in the centre of the door frame above the door, or on the ceiling. These devices detect movement, but not stationary traffic. Motion sensors will not prevent a door from closing if a person is positioned in the path of the door leaf and may not be able to detect people who are moving slowly in the doorway. They should therefore not be relied on as a safety override device (see p 9 *Safety devices*).

Presence sensor – These devices are typically infrared, but may also be ultrasonic or capacitive types, and operate by detecting movement and objects within a detection area. Presence sensors are able to detect stationary objects and people who are

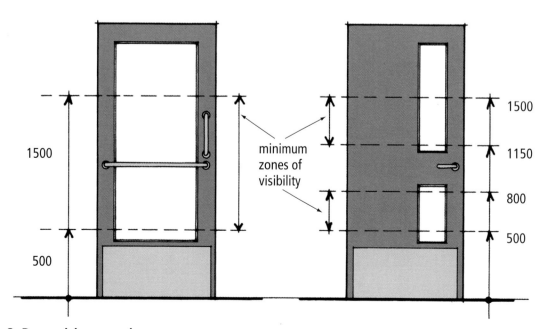

*Figure 2 **Door vision panels***

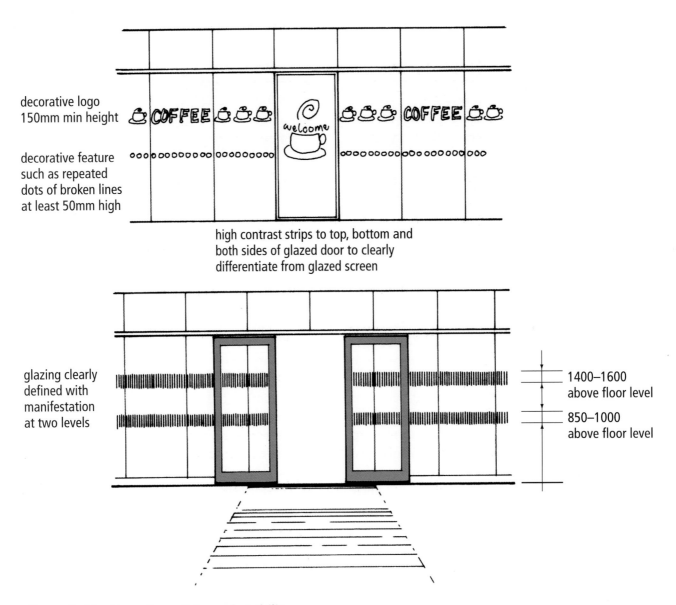

decorative logo
150mm min height

decorative feature
such as repeated
dots of broken lines
at least 50mm high

high contrast strips to top, bottom and
both sides of glazed door to clearly
differentiate from glazed screen

glazing clearly
defined with
manifestation
at two levels

1400–1600
above floor level

850–1000
above floor level

Figure 3 **Markings for safety and visibility**

moving slowly, and are therefore suitable for use as safety as well as activation devices.

The position and setting of any automatic activation device is critical to the effective

functioning and safety of the door and in ensuring the intended flow of pedestrians is achieved.

Safety devices

Safety devices are essential for doors with automatic systems and should ensure that a person does not become trapped or pushed by any moving components. The door activation

Motion sensor device

Presence sensor device

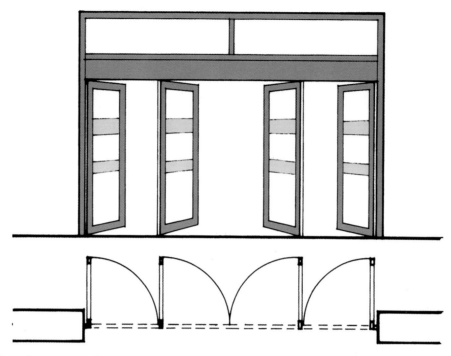

Figure 4 **Sliding doorset and side screens in break-out position**

devices can be used as safety devices if they are able to detect stationary objects. Alternatively, additional safety features may be added, depending on the type of installation and expected use.

Presence sensing devices – These are the preferred type of safety device because they are able to interrupt door movement at any point during the door movement cycle if a person remains in the door opening. Presence sensors are able to detect stationary objects, and should therefore prevent doors from moving in the event that a person falls within the doorway.

Passive safety devices – These include safety switches and pressure sensitive strips which, when contacted, prevent further movement of the door or a reversal of door movement.

Emergency escape

Doors fitted with automatic operating systems may be designated as emergency exit routes. If so, they should be fitted with one of the following systems:

- a manual break-out facility which enables the doors to swing open in the direction of escape, or

- a linkage to the fire alarm system, set to incorporate a monitored fail-safe system – that is, the doors to open in the event that the alarm is activated or the power fails

Break-out facilities typically require considerable force to swing the door or screen open. BS 7036-1 recommends an upper resistance limit of 220 newtons at the leading edge of the door. A resistance of this magnitude is likely to present considerable difficulties for mobility impaired people and people with reduced strength. Nonetheless, it is unlikely that the resistance can be significantly reduced, as to do so would undermine the nature and integrity of the door and framing in its intended sliding or folding arrangement.

It is therefore essential that building occupiers and managers ensure that there are adequate procedures in place to ensure the safe evacuation of all building users in the event of an emergency. This may involve the provision of assistance wherever a break-out facility is in place[1].

---

[1] It is the responsibility of the building occupier to ensure that adequate procedures are in place to facilitate safe egress for all building occupants in the event of an emergency.

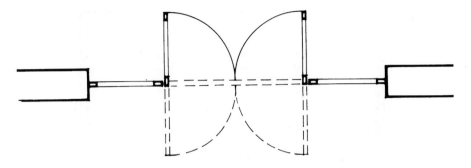

automatic swing doors which normally open
inwards can be set to open in direction of
escape by incorporating 'break-out' facility

Figure 5 **Swing door break-out**

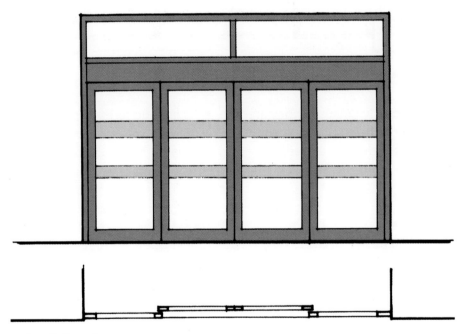

Bi-parting straight sliding door

Technical guidelines

This section covers design, installation and
safety considerations relevant to the following
types of automatic doors: sliding doors, swing
doors and balanced doors, low-energy swing
doors, and revolving doors.

Sliding doors

- **Single, bi-parting and telescopic straight
  sliding doors** – These doors can be used
  to maximise the available opening width at
  entrance doors; they avoid the need for deep
  lobby areas required by swing doors.

- **Single and bi-parting curved sliding doors
  and prismatic doors** – These doors require
  less width but greater lobby depth than a
  comparable straight sliding door.
- **Folding doors** – These doors are particularly
  useful for locations where space is limited
  and sideways sliding or swing doors are not
  appropriate.

The control system to sliding doors can be set
to automatic (normal daytime operation), off
(doors closed and operable only using a night
bank switch), exit only, permanently open or
partial opening. The partial opening setting
may be termed 'winter setting' because it
limits the door opening to a reduced width for

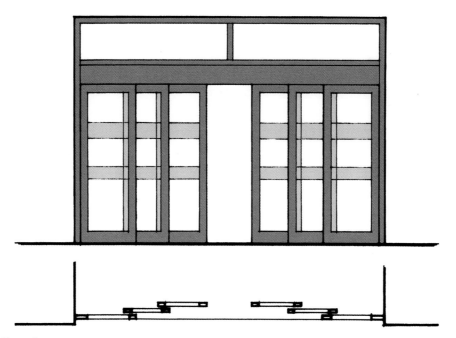

Telescopic sliding door

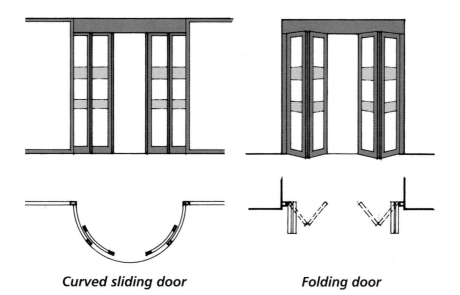

Curved sliding door   *Folding door*

the purpose of reducing heat loss or the ingress of rain and wind. Depending on the size of the door, partial opening may result in a door opening width which is difficult to access.

- Partial opening of sliding doors should not be used on narrow door openings. The opening mechanism should be set to provide a minimum clear opening width of 1000mm.

Sliding doors can present a potential risk to building users by creating finger or body traps, for example between the sliding door and fixed door frame, between

any static and fixed framing members, and between the outer edge of the sliding door and any return wall. The risk can be minimised by ensuring that potential traps are avoided.

- The distance between the sliding door leaf and any screen or barrier rail or element of building structure across which it slides should be designed to eliminate potential finger and body traps.
- Potential finger traps can be avoided by ensuring that any gaps between the sliding door, fixed framing members and barriers are greater than 25mm (see *Figure 6*).

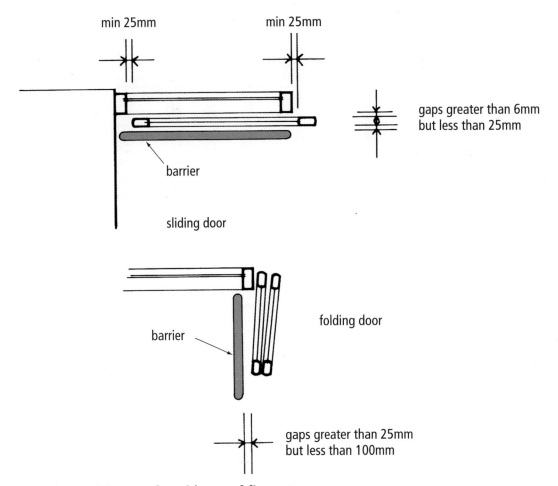

min 25mm   min 25mm

gaps greater than 6mm
but less than 25mm

barrier

sliding door

barrier

folding door

gaps greater than 25mm
but less than 100mm

Figure 6 **Barrier positions and avoidance of finger traps**

- Potential body traps can be avoided by achieving the dimensions in *Figure 7*.
- On folding doors, finger guards should be incorporated to either fill or minimise potential finger traps – this is particularly relevant to the pivot or junction point of the folding door leaf and to the junction between the hinge and the leading stile. Potential finger traps between the moving door leaves and any wall or barriers should be avoided (see *Figure 6*).

If people are unfamiliar with a building, unforeseen movement of an automatic door may be disconcerting. The visible features of an automatic operating system, such as overhead presence detectors, barrier rails and sliding tracks, will assist identification. In addition, automatic doors should be clearly identified with appropriate signage.

- A 'keep clear' sign should be affixed to the screen or wall across which the door travels.

Straight sliding door

Two curved bi-parting sliding doorsets forming lobby

Bi-parting folding door

Swing doors and balanced doors

Automatic swing doors can be installed in internal and exterior locations as part of new building work, or as operating units retrofitted to existing doorsets. Automatic swing doors can comprise single or double doorsets, installed in isolation, in pairs to form a lobby, or adjacent to each other to maximise circulation width.

Balanced doors combine a sliding and swing action. They typically comprise two bi-parting leaves, and provide the additional benefit of space saving.

Swing doors fitted with automatic opening devices swing in one direction only, but can be approached by pedestrians from one or both sides of the door. As the path of the door leaf (or leaves) moves across the pedestrian route, clear signage is essential to highlight the presence of the doors and their movement.

- One-way doors (for example, entrance only or exit only) should have a 'direction of travel' sign and an *Automatic door* sign on the approach side and a *No entry* and *Keep clear* sign on the reverse side.
- Two-way doors should have an *Automatic door* sign on both sides of the door and a *Keep clear* sign on the side which opens towards the user.

Where swing or balanced doors can be approached from the side, a barrier should be

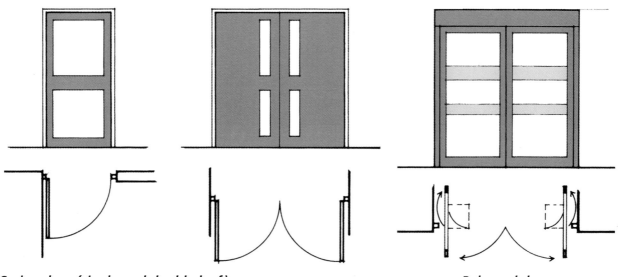

Swing door (single and double leaf)   *Balanced door*

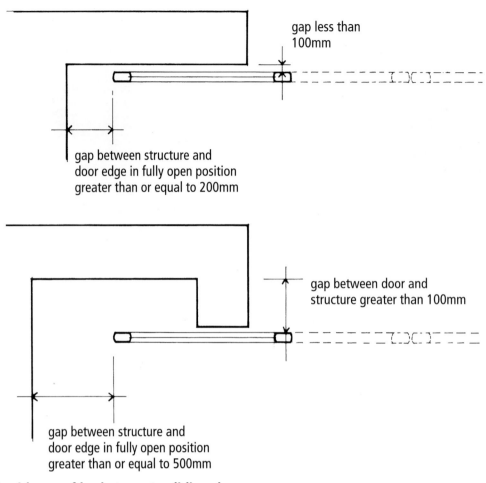

gap less than 100mm

gap between structure and door edge in fully open position greater than or equal to 200mm

gap between door and structure greater than 100mm

gap between structure and door edge in fully open position greater than or equal to 500mm

Figure 7 **Avoidance of body traps to sliding doors**

provided to prevent pedestrians from moving into or being struck by the door. Guards to prevent fingers being trapped between the door edge and frame are also required.

- Barriers should be at least 900mm high and visually distinguishable against the

surrounding surfaces. As with any guarding, the design should limit the likelihood of children being able to climb the guarding or become trapped.

- Finger traps should be avoided by ensuring there is a gap of at least 25mm but no greater than 50mm between the barrier rail

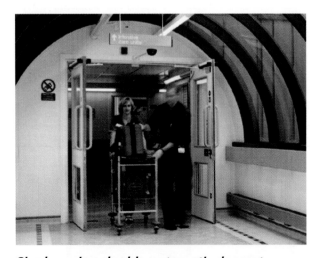

Single-swing double automatic doorset

Single-swing double and single doorsets for one-way traffic

Bi-parting balanced door

and the door in the fully open position (see *Figure 7*).

- Finger guards should be fitted to swing doors to prevent fingers from being trapped between the door edge and frame. This applies equally to new doors and existing doors being retro-fitted with automatic or low-energy operators.

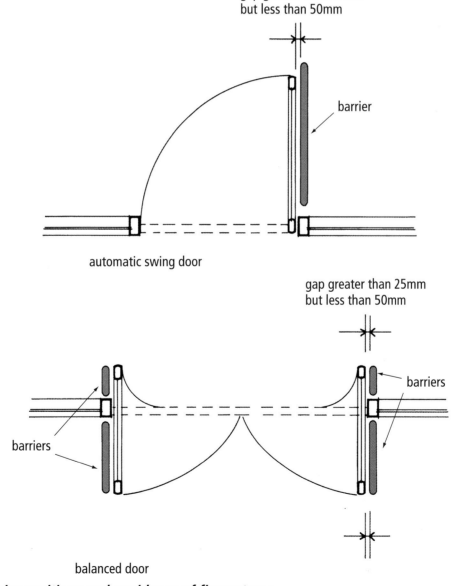

gap greater than 25mm but less than 50mm

barrier

automatic swing door

gap greater than 25mm but less than 50mm

barriers

barriers

balanced door

*Figure 8 **Barrier positions and avoidance of finger traps***

Low-energy swing doors

Low-energy swing doors allow the door to be used as a conventional manual door. However, the door can also be automatically opened when activated by those who require assistance. There are two main methods of activation:

- **power-assisted operation** in which the initiating signal is provided by the action of pushing, pulling or touching the door leaf or handle; or
- **power operation** in which the initiating signal is provided by a manual or automatic activation device. Individual manual activation devices include wall or post-mounted push pads, swipe card, proximity card and keypad devices. Doors can also be activated using remote control transmitters which can be hand held or mounted on a wheelchair.

The operating system is accommodated in an overhead box similar to, but much larger than, a conventional door-closing device.

The controls for manually activated doors should be accessible.

Wall-mounted push-pad door-opening device

- Wall- or post-mounted push pads should be located at a height between 750mm and 1000mm above floor level.
- Swipe card devices should be positioned vertically and within a range of 800mm to 1100mm above floor level (950mm to 1000mm preferred).
- Where possible, on the opening side of the door, manual activation devices should be set back 1400mm from the leading edge of the door so that the person using the device does not have to move clear of the door swing as it opens.
- Manual activation controls should contrast in colour and luminance with the background surfaces so that they are readily identifiable.

Door safety

Low-energy swing doors are not normally required to be fitted with safety devices because the speed of movement and door mass are not considered to present a significant hazard. The speed and mass combine, by calculation, to give a value for the kinetic energy of the door which is subject to a maximum value of 1.6 joules (BS 7036-4).

- The door speed should be adjusted so that it does not exceed the maximum permitted level. Heavier doors will require a slower speed and increased opening time.

The potential for people becoming trapped by the force of the closing door should be considered. Under BS 7036-4, the maximum permitted static entrapment force is 67 newtons when applied at a point 25mm from the leading of the door.

- If it is judged that the force of the door-closing mechanism is likely to present a risk to building users, or that any contact between the door leaf and a person moving through the door should be avoided, the use of a presence-sensing safety device should be considered.

Where a low-energy door swing can be approached from the side when the door is

Large revolving door with adjacent accessible automatic sliding door

open, a barrier should be provided to prevent pedestrians from moving into or being struck by the door.

- Barriers should be at least 900mm high and visually distinguishable against the surrounding surfaces.
- A gap of 25–50mm should be maintained between the door in the fully open position and the barrier (see *Figure 7*).
- As with any guarding, the design should limit the likelihood of children being able to climb the guarding or of becoming trapped.

Emergency exit

If low-energy swing doors are installed on emergency exit routes, the doors should be capable of being manually opened in the direction of escape. BS 7036-4 recommends that the opening force for manual opening should not exceed 90 newtons, which is less than the

upper limit for the break-out force for automatic doors, but still substantial and likely to present difficulties to many building users, including mobility impaired people and people with reduced strength.

- Building occupiers should ensure that procedures are in place which will facilitate the safe evacuation of all building users. This may involve the provision of an alternative, more accessible exit route or the provision of assistance in door opening.

In the event of a power failure, low-energy swing doors should be capable of manual operation when a force of 90 newtons is applied to the leading edge of the door. Again, this force is likely to present difficulties to many people, and measures should be in place to ensure either that an alternative route is available or that assistance can be provided with door opening.

Revolving doors

Revolving doors are not considered accessible, and present particular difficulties to ambulant disabled people, visually impaired people, people with assistance dogs, and people with young children or pushchairs. Large-diameter revolving doors, which are common in large stores, offer greater space in each compartment and are relatively slow moving, but still present risks to disabled users. The use of glass panels enclosing and adjacent to revolving doors can be confusing, particularly to visually impaired people. In such situations, it is essential that the presence of the glass is clearly highlighted with manifestation markings.

If the use of a revolving door cannot be avoided, it is essential that an alternative accessible door is provided immediately adjacent to the revolving door, and that it is available for use at all times. The accessible door could be a swing, sliding or folding door and be automatic, manual or power operated. The door should be clearly identified and signed to show that it is accessible.

Building management

Operation and maintenance

Automatic door systems are legally required by the Provision and Use of Work Equipment Regulations 1998 to be serviced periodically and in accordance with the criteria set out in BS 7036. This is to ensure that the door systems are safe, secure and remain fully operational.

BS 7036 recommends that powered doors are maintained regularly to manufacturers' specifications by authorised technicians. Copies of checklists completed during the installation and site acceptance test and subsequent annual inspections should be retained by both the authorised technician and the building owner or manager.

The Automatic Door Suppliers' Association (ADSA) sets a competency exam which, after successful completion, shows that the servicing or installation engineer is knowledgeable about the requirements of BS 7036.

Authorised technician inspections

When automatic door systems are installed, they are subject to an installation and site acceptance test, which should be carried out by an authorised technician. Automatic door systems should also undergo an annual inspection, again carried out by an authorised technician, in order to ensure ongoing safety and efficient operation. The test records data about the door, including door mechanism opening and closing times, the hold-open time, closing energies, activation distances, safety devices (type, position and number), door protection, emergency escape features and signage.

Occupier safety checks

The building manager or occupier responsible for building maintenance should carry out regular safety checks of the door and its operating system. The detailed content of the checklist will depend on the type of automatic door system, but will include the following general categories:

- automatic activation devices
- safety devices
- general tests

The frequency of occupier safety checks will depend on the type of installation and the frequency of use. This should be determined with reference to the Hazard Analysis and Risk Assessment which should be undertaken in the initial design and specification stages in order to identify the most appropriate type and size of door for the intended use.

Case studies

St Monica's Hospital, Easingwold

Two automatic bi-parting sliding door systems were used at St Monica's Hospital to provide easy access for staff, visitors and patients through a new entrance lobby, constructed as part of the hospital's Millennium Project. The automatic sliding doors were installed within a hardwood glazed structure that forms a lobby and waiting area. The sliding door leaves are white and provide effective contrast with the dark timber-framed lobby structure. This maximises visibility and highlights the location of the entrance.

The space available for constructing the new lobby was limited, and sliding doors were selected as they required less lobby depth than swing doors. Sliding doors were also considered to present less of a hazard in terms of door movement than swing doors. The provision of two sets of doors helps to minimise the loss of internal warm air.

The glazed waiting area inside the lobby has proved a popular year-round sitting area for ambulant patients. The area is cool on summer mornings and also gets some afternoon sun. The lobby provides a pleasant environment in the winter when it is heated and receives maximum daylight.

The automatic sliding-door systems provide easy access into and out of the hospital entrance and maximise circulation space in the lobby. The entrance provides an attractive seating area for patients and visitors

Chichester Police Station

Police stations can be forbidding buildings, particularly if the necessary security measures seem designed to keep people out. However, as public buildings, police stations should be accessible to all members of the public. A recently installed automatic door system has helped Chichester Police Station in West Sussex transform its 'front of house' to make the front office, counters and screens more accessible and welcoming to visitors.

Chichester Police Station

The folding-door arrangement to the main public entrance was selected because it suited the restricted lobby and foyer space and maximised the clear door-opening width

The police station has been extensively refurbished to improve both accessibility and security. The front office is now accessed via a new automatic folding door, which was installed within an existing wall opening. The new doors allow more light into the building and improve its ambience.

Folding doors are ideal for installation in existing door openings, across corridors or in limited spaces where it would be difficult to fit other types of automatic doors owing to limitations in space.

The new custody units behind the main office are now accessed by sliding doors fitted with automatic modular sliding-door operators. This type of operator is suitable for use with almost all sliding door types. The range is versatile, being equally suitable for light interior doors and heavy external and escape route doors.

Disability Rights Commission, London

The Disability Rights Commission (DRC) installed a number of automatic door systems at its new London headquarters in Gray's Inn Road. The DRC office was extensively refurbished prior to occupation and equipped with a range of different automatic door systems to provide easy access throughout the building.

Low-energy swing-door operators, which are designed specifically to provide easier access for people through doors which would otherwise be fairly heavy to operate, have been installed to the office, lobby and room doors. These doors can be equipped with a range of operating modes to allow the door to be opened under power when required, used manually at other times, or set to allow

The office entrance comprises an automatic bi-parting doorset with fully glazed doors. The presence of glass has been highlighted with two contrasting bands across each door leaf incorporating the DRC logo

permanent, automatic-powered operation. The low-energy door operators at the DRC are all fitted with wall or barrier-mounted push pads.

The WC lobby and office doors have been equipped with low-energy door operators. The push-pad activation devices are visible on the barrier rails and the wall adjacent to the reception desk

Appendices

Glossary

Door type definitions

Balanced door
A power-operated door equipped with double-pivot hardware which causes the door to open with a combined sliding and swing action.

Automatic bi-parting sliding door
A power-operated door which has two door leaves opening away from each other.

Automatic folding door
A power-operated door comprising two or more door leaves hinged together and with one door leaf side-hung to the door frame.

Automatic revolving door
A powered door with two or more door leaves which rotate around a central axis. Revolving doors can vary greatly in size and speed of operation.

Automatic sliding door
A powered door which has one or more door leaves that move sideways across an opening.

Automatic swing door
A powered door which is hinged on one vertical edge (or near to the edge) and swings open in one direction.

Automatic telescopic sliding door
A powered sliding door with two or more leaves which move telescopically across an opening.

Automatic prismatic door
A powered bi-parting sliding door which has two leaves that meet at an angle to one another.

Low-energy swing door
A swing door fitted with a power-operated opening device which can be set to provide powered opening assistance. The initiating signal can be provided by the action of pushing, pulling or touching the door leaf or handle, or by a manually operated or automatic activation device.

Building Regulations

England and Wales

In England and Wales, building design and construction is governed by the Building Regulations. These regulations comprise a series of requirements for specific purposes: health and safety, energy conservation, prevention of contamination of water, and the welfare and convenience of persons in or about buildings.

Part M – Part M of the regulations sets minimum legal standards for access to and use of buildings by all building users, including disabled people. Since a requirement for access was first introduced in 1985, there have been a number of changes to and extensions in the scope of access regulations. The most recent – and most radical – revision came into effect on 1 May 2004. Whereas, previously, Part M was concerned with 'access for disabled people', now the requirement (for non-domestic buildings) is simply that:

- **Access and use**
  'Reasonable provision shall be made for people to gain access to and use the building and its facilities.'

This does not apply to any part of a building that is used solely to enable the building or any service or fitting within the building to be inspected, repaired or maintained.

- **Access to extensions to buildings**
  'Suitable independent access shall be provided to the extension where reasonably practicable.'

This does not apply where suitable access to the extension is provided throughout the building that is extended.

- **Sanitary conveniences in extensions to buildings**
  'If sanitary conveniences are provided in any building that is to be extended, reasonable provision shall be made within the extension for sanitary conveniences.'

This does not apply where there is reasonable provision for sanitary conveniences elsewhere in the building that can be accessed by building users.

The regulation avoids specific reference to, and a definition of, disabled people. This inclusive approach means that buildings and their facilities should be accessible to and usable by all people who use buildings – including parents with children, older people and disabled people. Previously, Part M covered new buildings and extensions to existing buildings. The 2004 revision brings Part M into line with other parts of the Building Regulations by extending its scope to include alterations to existing buildings and certain changes of use.

Approved Document M – Building Regulations are supported by 'Approved Documents' which give practical guidance with respect to the regulations. While their use is not mandatory – and the requirements of regulations can be met in other ways – Approved Documents are used as a benchmark by the local authority. The new Approved Document M (AD M), published in November 2003, offers technical guidance on providing access to and within buildings. It is informed by the relevant British Standard (BS 8300:2001 *Design of buildings and their approaches to meet the needs of disabled people – Code of practice*, see p 5), although the British Standard also contains guidance on issues that it is not appropriate or realistic to control under Building Regulations approval and inspection procedures, such as interior decoration and the selection of door ironmongery. Dimensional criteria in the new AD M are largely in accordance with BS 8300. Where there are differences, these result from accumulated experience fed back to the Government during its consultation on the new AD M. The guidance in AD M should be followed in preference to dimensional criteria in BS 8300. It is important that reference is made to AD M for details of the circumstances in which Part M applies and what provision is required.

Scotland

In Scotland, access requirements are integrated into general Technical Standards. These apply to: new buildings; conversions; extensions to existing buildings (but not to the existing buildings themselves); and parts of a building that are altered or that are adversely affected by an alteration being carried out elsewhere in the building. At the time of writing, the Building Regulations system is being modernised and Technical Standards are being reviewed.

Northern Ireland

In Northern Ireland, Part R of the Building Regulations (NI) covers Access and Facilities for Disabled People, and is supported by Technical Booklet R:2000.

Disability Discrimination Act 1995

The Disability Discrimination Act (DDA) introduced new measures aimed at ending the discrimination which many disabled people face. In addition to granting new rights to disabled people, the Act also places duties on, among others, employers (Part 2), providers of goods, facilities and services (Part 3), and education providers (Part 4).

The main thrust of the legislation is to improve access for disabled people to employment, education and services. While the DDA does not directly require accessible environments to be provided for disabled people, either in their place of work or for access to goods, facilities, or services (for example in shops, restaurants or offices to which the public have access), duties under the Act include the requirement to consider barriers created by physical features of buildings and to make adjustments in certain circumstances.

The Act defines a disabled person as 'someone who has a physical or mental impairment which has a substantial and long-term adverse effect on his or her ability to carry out normal day-to-day activities'. Discrimination occurs where without justification, and for a reason which relates to the disabled person's disability, a disabled person is treated less favourably than others to whom the reason does not or would not apply. Discrimination may also occur when there is a duty to make a reasonable adjustment and any failure to meet that duty cannot be justified.

Each Part of the DDA is supported by one or more Codes of Practice which give guidance on how to meet duties under the Act. While Codes of Practice neither impose legal obligations nor are authoritative statements of the law, they may be referred to in any legal proceedings pursued under the Act. Building designers, while not legally required to respond to the DDA, should anticipate the requirements of the Act by presuming that employees, students and customers will fit the definition of 'disabled person' under the Act, and design buildings accordingly. Those commissioning new buildings or adaptations to existing buildings should consider the implications of the DDA in terms of their ability to employ and offer services to disabled people on an equal basis.

The DDA applies to the whole of the UK, including (with modifications) Northern Ireland.

DDA Part 2: Employment

Employers have a duty not to treat disabled people less favourably than others for a reason relating to their disability, unless this can be justified, and to make adjustments to assist disabled employees or applicants for employment. This may involve changing physical features of the premises if these put a disabled person at a substantial disadvantage in comparison with persons who are not disabled. The duty of provision of a reasonable adjustment is triggered when an individual

disabled person applies for a job, is employed, or it becomes apparent that an existing employee requires some form of adjustment; there is no general or anticipatory duty under Part 2 to make provision for disabled people.

Duties in Part 2 of the DDA covering employers were introduced in December 1996 and have subsequently been amended under the Equal Treatment Directive, which implements obligations placed by the European Union on the UK in relation to disability discrimination. From 1 October 2004, the Directive brought into effect the removal of the existing exemption for small employers so that the Part 2 duties relate to all employers. The Directive has also changed the relationship between the Building Regulations and Part 2 of the DDA. The partial exemption from the duty to remove or alter physical features which applies to service providers under Part 3 of the Act no longer applies to employers under Part 2.

DDA Part 3: Service provision

Part 3 of the DDA places duties on those providing goods, facilities or services to the public ('service providers') and those selling, letting or managing premises. The Act makes it unlawful for service providers, landlords and other persons to discriminate against disabled people in certain circumstances.

The duties on service providers have been introduced in three stages:

- Since December 1996, it has been unlawful for service providers to treat disabled people less favourably for a reason related to their disability.
- Since October 1999, service providers have had to make 'reasonable adjustments' for disabled people, such as providing extra help or making changes to the way they provide their services, or overcoming physical barriers by providing a service by a reasonable alternative method.
- From October 2004, service providers may have to make other 'reasonable adjustments' in relation to the physical

features of their premises to overcome physical barriers to access.

The *Code of Practice Rights of Access: Goods, Facilities, Services and Premises*, published by the Disability Rights Commission in 2002, outlines what may be considered as reasonable for disabled people to establish rights of access to goods, facilities, services and premises. Several factors have a bearing on whether a change is a reasonable one to make: effectiveness; practicality; cost and disruption; and financial resources.

DDA Part 4: Education

The Special Educational Needs and Disability Act 2001 (SENDA) amended Part 4 of the DDA and expanded the duties relating to disabled pupils and students. Education providers are now required to make 'reasonable adjustments' for disabled students and pupils. The duties cover all areas of education, schools, colleges, universities, adult education and youth services, including:

- not to treat disabled students or pupils less favourably than non-disabled students or pupils without justification
- to make reasonable adjustments to policies, practices and procedures that may discriminate against disabled students or pupils
- to provide education by a 'reasonable alternative means' where a physical feature places a disabled student/pupil at a substantial disadvantage
- a duty on local education authorities in England and Wales to plan strategically and increase the overall accessibility to school premises and the curriculum (a similar duty is placed on authorities in Scotland under the Education (Disability Strategies and Pupils' Education Records) (Scotland) Act 2002)

Additional duties placed on providers of post-16 education are as follows:

- from September 2002: not to discriminate against existing and prospective disabled students by treating them less favourably in the provision of student services

- from September 2003: to make reasonable adjustments to provide auxiliary aids
- from September 2005: to make adjustments to physical features. This is an anticipatory and continuing duty

Many schools or further/higher education providers are also service providers (for example where premises are used for evening classes, exhibitions or parents' evenings) and therefore also have duties under Part 3.

Sources of useful information

Organisations

Automatic Door Suppliers Association
411 Limpsfield Road
The Green
Warlingham
Surrey CR6 9HA
Tel: 01883 624961
Fax: 01883 626841
Email: admin@adsa.org.uk
Website: www.adsa.org.uk

Promotes standards of safety, quality, reliability and after-sales service.

British Standards Institution (BSI)
389 Chiswick High Road
London W4 4AL
Tel: 020 8996 9000
Fax: 020 8996 7001
Email: cservices@bsi-global.com
Website: www.bsi.org.uk

Publishes British Standards including BS 8300:2001 *Design of buildings and their approaches to meet the needs of disabled people – Code of practice*.

Centre for Accessible Environments
70 South Lambeth Road
London SW8 1RL
Tel/textphone: 020 7840 0125
Fax: 020 7840 5811
Email: info@cae.org.uk
Website: www.cae.org.uk

Provides technical information, training and consultancy on making buildings accessible to all users, including disabled and older people and carers of young children.

Construction Products Association
26 Store Street
London WC1E 7BT
Tel: 020 7323 3770
Fax: 020 7323 0307
Email: enquiries@constprod.org.uk
Website: www.constprod.org.uk

Trade association representing manufacturers and suppliers of construction products, components and fittings.

Department of Finance and Personnel
Building Regulations Unit
Third Floor, Lancashire House
3 Linenhall Street
Belfast BT2 8AA
Tel: 028 90542923
Email: DFP.enquiries@dfpni.gov.uk
Website: www2.dfpni.gov.uk

For information on the Northern Ireland Technical Booklets.

Disability Rights Commission
DRC Helpline
Freepost MID 02164
Stratford-upon-Avon CV37 9BR
Tel: 08457 622 633
Textphone: 08457 622 644
Fax: 08457 778 878
Email: enquiry@drc-gb.org
Website: www.drc.org.uk

Publishes codes of practice and other guidance related to the DDA.

The Equality Commission for Northern Ireland
Equality House
7–9 Shaftesbury Square
Belfast BT2 7DP
Tel: 028 90 500600
Fax: 028 90 248687
Textphone: 028 90 500589
Email: information@equalityni.org

Works towards the elimination of discrimination and keeps the relevant legislation under review.

Royal Institute of British Architects (RIBA)
66 Portland Place
London W1B 1AD
Public information line: 0906 302 0400
Tel: 020 7580 5533
Fax: 020 7255 1541
Email: info@inst.riba.org
Website: www.architecture.com

The RIBA advances architecture by demonstrating benefit to society and excellence in the profession.

Scottish Executive Development Department
Victoria Quay
Edinburgh EH6 6QQ
Tel: 0131 556 8400
Textphone: 0131 244 1829
Fax: 0131 244 8240
Email: ceu@scotland.gov.uk
Website: www.scotland.gov.uk

For information on the Scottish Technical Standards.

The Stationery Office Ltd
PO Box 29
Duke Street
Norwich NR3 1GN
Tel: 0870 600 5522
Fax: 0870 600 5533
Email: services@tso.co.uk
Online ordering:
www.tso.co.uk/bookshop

Sells printed versions of any item of legislation or any other official publication previously published by HMSO.

Publications

Legislation, standards and codes of practice

The Building Regulations 2000
Approved Document M: Access to and use of buildings (England and Wales)
Office of the Deputy Prime Minister
The Stationery Office, 2003

The Building Regulations (Northern Ireland) 2000 Technical booklet R: Access and facilities for disabled people
Great Britain Department of Finance and Personnel (Northern Ireland)
The Stationery Office, 2001

Scottish Executive Technical Standard, 6th Amendment
Scottish Executive
The Stationery Office, 2001

BS 5588-8:1999 Fire precautions in the design, construction and use of buildings – Code of practice for means of escape for disabled people
British Standards Institution, 1999

BS 8300:2001 Design of buildings and their approaches to meet the needs of disabled people – Code of practice
British Standards Institution, 2001

Code of Practice Rights of Access to Goods, Facilities, Services and Premises
Disability Rights Commission
The Stationery Office, 2002

Code of Practice for providers of Post-16 education and related services
Disability Rights Commission
The Stationery Office, 2002

Code of Practice for Schools
Disability Rights Commission
The Stationery Office, 2002

Code of Practice – Employment and Occupation
Disability Rights Commission
The Stationery Office, 2004

Code of Practice – Trade Organisations and Qualification Bodies
Disability Rights Commission
The Stationery Office, 2004

Provision and Use of Work Equipment Regulations 1998
The Stationery Office, 1998

Other publications

Access for Disabled People
Sport England, 2002
Design guidance note including a series of checklists for auditing sports buildings.

Building Sight
by Peter Barker, Jon Barrick, Rod Wilson
HMSO in association with the Royal National Institute of the Blind
RNIB, 1995
A handbook of building and interior design solutions to include the needs of visually impaired people.

Designing for Accessibility
CAE/RIBA Enterprises, 2004
Up-to-date and user-friendly good practice guide based on the 2004 Approved Document M and BS 8300:2001

A Design Guide for the Use of Colour and Contrast to Improve the Built Environment for Visually Impaired People
Dulux Technical Group, ICI Paints, 1997

Disabled Access to Facilities: a practical and comprehensive guide to a service provider's duties under Part III (2004) of the Disability Discrimination Act 1995
FM Law Series
by Ian Waterman and Janet A Bell,
Access Matters UK Ltd
Butterworths Tolley Lexis Nexis, 2002

Inclusive School Design – Accommodating pupils with special educational needs and disabilities in mainstream schools
Department for Education and Employment
The Stationery Office, 2001

Sign Design Guide
by Peter Parker and June Fraser
JMU and the Sign Design Society, 2000
A guide to inclusive signage.